Penguins

Shelby Braidich

Rosen
REAL
READERS

Rosen Classroom Books and Materials
New York

Penguins are birds.

Penguins cannot fly.

Penguins can swim.

Most penguins are black and white.

Penguins eat fish.

Baby penguins are chicks.

Words to Know

black

chicks

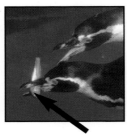

fish

swim

white